ABC

Costume and Textiles from the Los Angeles County Museum of Art

Florence Cassen Mayers

Harry N. Abrams, Inc.
Publishers
New York

For Aunt Ruthy and Uncle Sidney Trohn

Editor: Harriet Whelchel
Designer: Florence Cassen Mayers
Picture and Caption Research: Louise Coffey, Department of Costume and Textiles,
    Los Angeles County Museum of Art
Photography: Barbara Lyter, Department of Photographic Services,
    Los Angeles County Museum of Art

Library of Congress Cataloging-in-Publication Data
Mayers, Florence Cassen.
ABC, costume and textiles from the Los Angeles County Museum of Art/
Florence Cassen Mayers.
p.   cm.
Summary: Presents, in alphabetical order, examples of various items of familiar and
unusual items of clothing from the Los Angeles County Museum.
ISBN 0–8109–1877–3: $9.95
1. Costume—Juvenile literature. 2. Los Angeles County Museum of Art—Juvenile
literature. [1. Costume. 2. Los Angeles County Museum of Art. 3. Museums.
4. Alphabet.] I. Los Angeles County Museum of Art. II. Title. III. Title: A.B.C.,
costume and textiles from the Los Angeles County Museum of Art. IV. Title:
Costume and textiles from the Los Angeles County Museum of Art.
GT518.M39 1988
391—dc19
[E]   88–6163
            CIP
            AC

Design copyright © 1988 Florence Cassen Mayers
Photographs copyright © 1988 by Museum Associates,
Los Angeles County Museum of Art

Published in 1988 by Harry N. Abrams, Incorporated, New York.

A Times Mirror Company

Printed and bound in Japan

Other Books in the ABC Series
ABC: Museum of Fine Arts, Boston
ABC: The Museum of Modern Art, New York
ABC: The National Air and Space Museum
ABC: Egyptian Art from The Brooklyn Museum
ABC: Musical Instruments from The Metropolitan Museum of Art

Title page:
Edward MacKinder (English)
Sampler, 1878
Wool embroidery on linen canvas; 25 x 26″
Gift of Dr. and Mrs. Franklin Horowitz and Family

Introduction

In this unique and beautiful ABC, each letter of the alphabet is illustrated with selections from the collection of costume and textiles in the Los Angeles County Museum of Art. Represented here are only a few of the approximately 60,000 items in the Museum's collection, one that spans twenty-five hundred years and encompasses many cultures throughout the world. The examples in this book represent both the practical and the beautiful of earlier times, and most are chance survivals.

Velvet and beaded mittens, a straw top hat, and brocade shoes, easy to recognize, will delight even the youngest child. Older children will be intrigued to learn that the green and red platform shoe pictured in this book might have been worn by a father, or even a grandfather, in the early 1970s, or that the blue ostrich-feather hat was in style long ago, when great-great-grandmothers were young. And children of all ages will enjoy discovering new and different examples from other lands: the traditional dress of Japan, a kimono with embroidered poems; a bridal shoe from China; an elaborate English Renaissance glove, which was presented to nobility as a diplomatic gift; seventeenth-century gold and silver Italian lace.

Because of their fragile nature, historic dress, accessories, and textiles are displayed for no longer than three months at a time. It is the special privilege of this ABC to highlight a fabulous collection that is so carefully preserved and exhibited.

Aa

Apron

Apron
England, 1730–40
Silk taffeta, silk and metallic thread embroidery; 18 x 38″
Costume Council Fund

Bb

Boot

Woman's Boot
United States, c. 1910
Suede, patent-leather appliqué; height 11¾"
Promised Gift of Mrs. Charles D. Cline

Cape

Cape with Hood
France, c. 1780–90
Printed cotton (printed at Hausmann Factory in Colmar, Alsace);
center front 60"
Mrs. Alice F. Schott Bequest

Dd

Dress

Girl's Dress
United States, c. 1868–70
Wool twill, silk velvet ribbon and wool braid trim, faceted glass
buttons; center back 23¼″ (dress), center back 11¼″ (overskirt),
center back 10½″ (bolero)
Mrs. Alice F. Schott Bequest

Ee

Embroidery

Ff

Fan

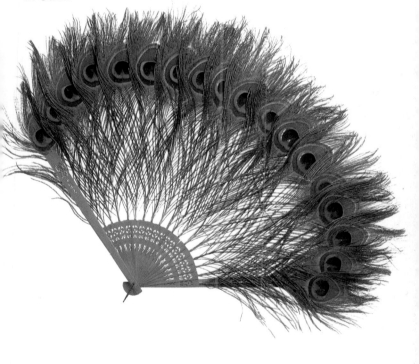

Altar Frontal (detail)
Italy (Venice), 1700–1725
Ribbed silk with metallic thread; silk, chenille, and metallic
thread embroidery; 24½ x 85¼"
Costume Council Needlework Fund

Fan
United States, c. 1920
Peacock feathers, carved wood; 17¾ x 25½"
Promised Gift of Mrs. Phillip Zobelin

Gg

Glove

Man's Glove
England, c. 1625–50
Leather, silk satin, silver gilt lace, silk embroidery, and spangles;
length 14″
Gift of Miss Margaret Isabel Fairfax MacKnight

Hh

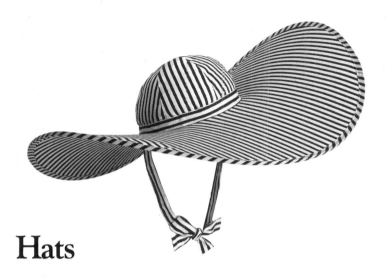

Hats

Collapsible Wide-Brimmed Sun Hat
United States, c. 1932
Cotton, with wire-brim support; width 23¼", depth 4¾"
From the Collection of Mme. Ganna Walska
Gift of Hania P. Tallmadge

Woman's Hat
United States, c. 1880
Silk velvet, metal brooch, ostrich-feather trim; 6 x 11"
Gift of Mrs. John Townsend Smith

Man's Hat
United States, c. 1832
Woven straw, grosgrain ribbon trim, silk lining; 7 x 12½"
Costume Council Curatorial Discretionary Fund

Ii

Iron

Henry Robert Morland (English, c. 1730–97)
The Laundry Maid, Ironing, c. 1785
Oil on canvas; 30 x 25″
Marion Davies Collection

Jj

Jewelry

William de Lillo (American, born Belgium, 1925)
Jewelry, 1971
Necklace: glass beads, faux diamonds, 18-karat gold
electroplated brass; length 22″
Brooch: Austrian glass beads, faux diamonds, 18-karat gold
electroplated brass; 4½ x 4″
Shell Gallery Belt: Austrian glass beads, turquoise stones,
faux diamonds, 18-karat gold electroplated brass; 30½ x 4″
Gift of William de Lillo and Robert F. Clark

Kk

Kimono

Kimono
Japan, early 19th century
Resist-dyed silk crepe, silk and gold thread embroidery, China
silk lining; center back 64½″
Gift of Miss Bella Mabury

Ll

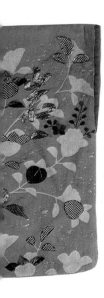

Lace

Table Cover (detail)
Italy [?], c. 1650
Gold, silver, and silk needle lace; 68 x 53¾"
Costume Council Fund

Mm

Mittens

Mitts
United States, c. 1835–40
Knitted cotton, glass and metallic beads; length 6¼"
Costume Council Fund

Mitts
United States, c. 1840
Silk velvet, silk thread embroidery, silk cord and tassels;
length 8¾"
Costume Council Fund

Nn

Nightwear

Negligee
United States, 1900–1910
Silk voile, cotton machine lace, silk taffeta interlining,
cotton net lining; center back 42″
Wilma Alice Leithead Wood Bequest

Oo

Overcoat

Man's Overcoat
United States, c. 1938
Camel-hair and wool, rayon lining; center back 45½″
Gift of Mrs. Joseph von Sternberg

Pp

Parasol

Parasol
United States [?], c. 1880
Silk damask, silk lace, silk ribbon trim, China silk lining,
carved wood handle; length 34″
Gift of Mrs. John Townsend Smith

Qq

Quilt

Quilt, *Full-Blown Tulip* (detail)
United States, c. 1830
Printed and plain cotton, pieced and quilted; 94⅛ x 92⅛″
Gift of The Betty Horton Collection

Rr

Ribbons

Ribbons (Folk)
Spain or France, early 19th century
Figured silk; length (*top* to *bottom*) 53¼″, 64⅜″, 46⅛″,
30⅛″, 32¼″
Gift of Mrs. Kathryn R. Stanley

Shoes

Woman's Shoe
England, c. 1720–30
Silk brocade, silk ribbon trim; 4 x 9″
Mrs. Alice R. Schott Bequest

Bridal Shoe
China, c. 1900–1940
Silk satin and damask, silk thread embroidery, cotton and
leather trim, and cotton muslin (covering stilt); 5 x 9½″
Wilma Alice Leithead Wood Bequest

Man's Platform Shoe
France, c. 1973
Leather, crepe rubber sole; 7½ x 10½″
Anonymous Gift

Stocking

Man's Stocking
India, first half 19th century
Knitted wool and metallic thread, silk tassels; 29⅞ x 7½"
Nasli and Alice Heeramaneck Collection
Museum Associates Purchase

Top: Fragment of Burial Mantle
Peru (Nazca), 900–1476
Wool and cotton, tapestry technique; 14½ x 18″
Costume Council and Museum Associates Funds

Tt

Tapestry

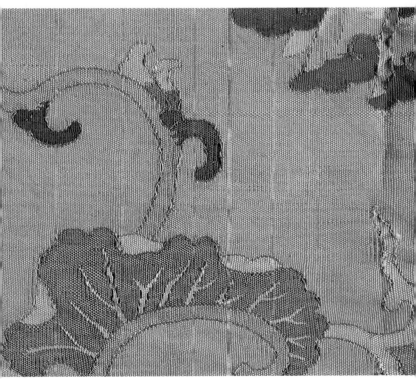

Emperor's Ceremonial Cape (detail of Hood)
China, 18th century (Ch'ien-lung dynasty)
Silk, tapestry technique; center back 55″
Gift of Miss Bella Mabury

Uu

Uniform

Woman's Uniform
United States, 1918
Wool twill, leather and metal trim; center back 28¼″ (jacket),
center back 28½″ (skirt), hat length 12″, belt length 35″
Gift of Mrs. Potter Bowles

Vv

Vest

Waistcoat
Spain, c. 1790
Silk satin, silk thread embroidery, linen lining;
center back 19¾″
Gift of Mrs. Norman Topping

la Cleopatre

la Daurienne

Wigs

Headdresses (detail)
France (Paris), 18th century
Engraving, hand tinted (watercolor); 11⅝ x 9⅜″
Costume Council Fund

Wedding gown

Benito (Edouardo Garcia, born Spain, active in France)
C'est L'aurore d'un beau jour, 1921
Fashion plate from *Gazette du Bon Ton,* no. 2, p. 40, plate 11
Pouchoir (hand stenciled); 7 x 5⅜"
Los Angeles County Museum of Art Library

Xx

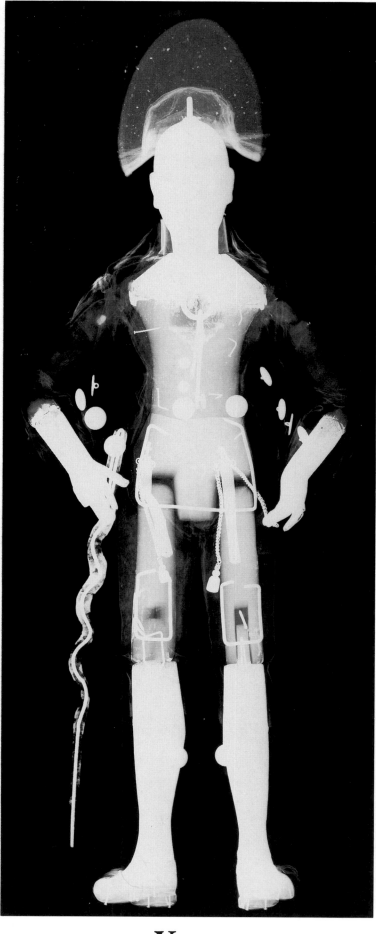

X-ray

X-ray of an *Incroyable* Doll
France, c. 1790
Doll: painted carved wood; costume: wool and silk; 23½ x 7″
Costume Council Fund

Yy

Yarn

Man's National Costume (detail)
Bolivia, c. 1930
Wool, applied yarn, cotton rickrack, rayon velvet trim;
center back 18¾"
Costume and Textile Department Fund

Zz

Zipper

Rudi Gernreich (American, 1922–85)
Woman's Sportswear Top (detail), c. 1966
Wool jersey, metal zipper; center back 29¾″
Gift of Jimmy M. Mitchell